# WHICH WAY TO THE MILKY WAY?

A Question of Science Book

# WHICH WAY TO THE MILKY WAY?

by Sidney Rosen
illustrated by Dean Lindberg

Carolrhoda Books, Inc. / Minneapolis

Each word that appears in **BOLD** in the text is explained in the glossary on page 40.

LIBRARY OF CONGRESS CATALOGING-IN-PUBLICATION DATA

Rosen, Sidney.
    Which way to the Milky Way? / by Sidney Rosen ; illustrated by Dean Lindberg.
        p.      cm. — (A Question of science book)
    Summary: Questions and answers introduce the Milky Way and other kinds of galaxies in the universe.
    ISBN 0-87614-709-0 (lib. bdg.)
    1. Milky Way—Miscellanea—Juvenile literature. 2. Galaxies—Miscellanea—Juvenile literature. [1. Milky Way—Miscellanea. 2. Galaxies—Miscellanea. 3. Questions and answers.] I. Lindberg, Dean, ill. II. Title. III. Series.
QB857.7.R67   1992
523.1'13—dc20                                      91-26748
                                                        CIP
                                                        AC

Manufactured in the United States of America

1  2  3  4  5  6  97  96  95  94  93  92

*What is the Milky Way, anyway?*

It's a wide band of stars that stretches across the sky at night.

*If it's made of stars, why is it called the Milky Way?*

6

Because you can't see the separate stars without a
**telescope.** To people living long before the telescope
was invented, the stars seemed to be a white band
across the sky. People in Greece made up a story that
this white band was a river of milk.

*What does the Milky Way have to do with us
on Earth?*

The Milky Way is part of a great collection of stars called a **galaxy**. Our Sun and all the planets that go around it are part of this galaxy. The word "galaxy" comes from the Greek word for milk: *gala.* The ancient Romans called the Milky Way *Via Galactica,* which means "the road made of milk."

*So we're part of the Milky Way galaxy?*

Yes.  The Sun, planets, and everything else in our **Solar System** are only a tiny part of the whole galaxy.

*But the Solar System is so large!  Aren't the farthest planets like Neptune and Pluto billions of miles away from Earth?*

Yes, they are. But when you think about the size of a galaxy, you have to use bigger numbers than that. You have to think **BIG**.

What's bigger than a billion? A zillion? A Dillion? A GAZILLION or a Megajillion? A KINGKONGZILLION? Maybe a HUMONGOSKWILLION? or a GIGAZILLION?

You have to give up thinking in miles altogether.

**Give up miles?  What will we use instead?**

Start thinking in terms of a beam of light traveling across a galaxy. The speed of light is about 186,000 miles per second. In one year, that beam of light will travel about six trillion miles! We call this distance one **light-year**.

*So when we talk about distances in galaxies, we have to use light-years?*

On the blackboard:

$$365$$
$$\times 24$$
$$\overline{\phantom{0}}$$
$$8{,}760$$
$$\times 60$$
$$\overline{\phantom{0}}$$
$$525{,}600$$
$$\times 60$$
$$\overline{\phantom{0}}$$
$$31{,}536{,}000$$
$$\times 186{,}000$$
$$\overline{\phantom{0}}$$
$$5{,}865{,}696{,}000{,}000 \text{ miles} = 1 \text{ light-year}$$

On the note:

*How can I figure out the number of miles in a light-year?*

An Earth year has 365 days, a day has 24 hours, each hour has 60 minutes, and each minute has 60 seconds. Multiply these all together and you get the number of seconds in a year. We know that light travels at an amazing speed of 186,000 miles per second. So multiply the number of seconds in a year by 186,000 and you'll get the number of miles in a light-year — about six *trillion* miles.

Right. Our Milky Way galaxy is 100,000 light-years across.

*Wow, that's big! Are we right in the center of the galaxy?*

13

No.  The Milky Way is a **spiral galaxy**.  It's shaped like a round ball in the center, with spiral arms coming out of and circling around the ball.  Our Solar System is in one of the spiral arms.

*Does the Solar System move around with that spiral arm?*

Yes.  All the spiral arms of the Milky Way are slowly circling about the center, and our Solar System moves along with them.

*If the Solar System is moving along with a spiral arm, why don't I feel dizzy?*

Because our Solar System and the Milky Way are so big, and we're so small. And because distances between things in space are so large. Suppose you were a fly trapped in a moving car. The car could travel for miles without your knowing that you were moving at all.

*So the Solar System must be like that car, right?*

BUZZZ...

That's right!  The circle that the Solar System makes—
with us in it—around the center of the Milky Way is so
huge that we don't notice the motion at all.

*How far are we from the center of the Milky Way?*

About 30,000 light-years.  Imagine that the center of
the Milky Way is the downtown part of a large city like
Chicago.  Then our Solar System would be in one of the
city's distant suburbs.

*What's the center of the Milky Way like?*

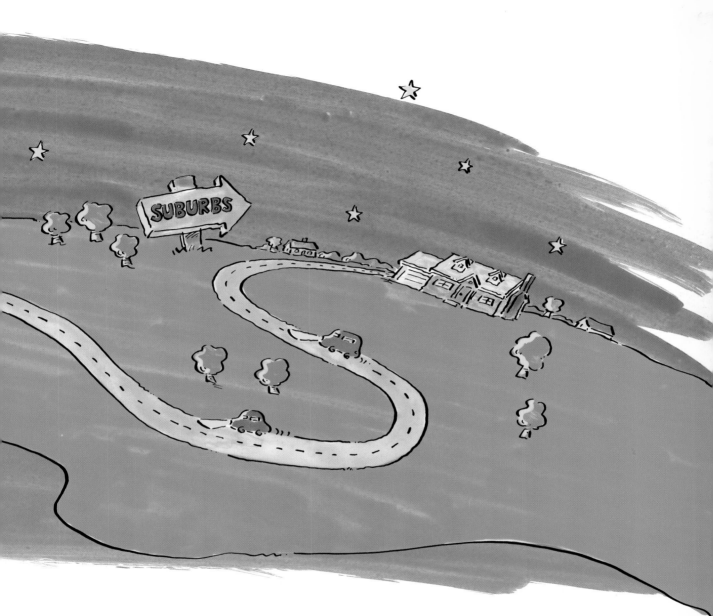

It's jammed so full of stars, that if you lived near the center, the sky would never get dark.

*When we see the band of the Milky Way in the sky at night, are we looking at the center of the galaxy?*

No. You're looking at one of the spiral arms. Which arm you see depends on the time of year and the direction in which you're looking.

*How many stars are there in the Milky Way?*

About 100 billion stars! If you tried to count them one by one, it would take you over three thousand years to finish! And if we could glue all the different stars in the Milky Way together, we'd wind up with a superstar 200 billion times bigger than our Sun!

**What keeps all the stars in a galaxy together?**

The same force that keeps us stuck to the Earth—
**gravity**. In a galaxy, gravity keeps the stars from
dashing away into outer space.

**Why don't the stars in the center of a galaxy bump into each other?**

The force of gravity makes objects move toward each other. You might expect such large objects as stars to move toward each other pretty quickly. But gravity acts between *all* the stars in a galaxy. So, while one star is being attracted to another, the attraction of a third star may be keeping the first two apart. Gravity keeps all the stars in a galaxy moving around, but the chances of one star bumping into another are pretty small. In the Milky Way galaxy, gravity keeps the stars in motion around each other. So there's no danger that our star, the Sun, will bump into another star.

*Is the Milky Way the only galaxy in the universe?*

No, there are hundreds of thousands of galaxies
scattered all through space. **Astronomers** think that
there may be about 100 billion galaxies altogether.
Some of the distant galaxies may be so far away that
their light never gets to our telescopes.

*Are any of them near us?*

Yes, if by "near" you mean inside a circle that's about three million light-years across. There are about 24 galaxies besides the Milky Way in this circle. Astronomers call this bunch of galaxies the Local Group. For fun, some call it the Local Swimming Hole.

*What's the nearest galaxy to us?*

Two galaxies, called the Large and Small Magellanic Clouds, are slowly going around the Milky Way. You can see these galaxies with the naked eye if you live south of the Earth's equator. When the Portuguese sea captain Ferdinand Magellan sailed around the world more than 400 years ago, his crew spotted those galaxies.

*How far away from us are the Magellanic Clouds?*

The Large Cloud is 160,000 light-years away from the center of the Milky Way. The Small Cloud is about 200,000 light-years away.

*You call that close?*

For galaxies, yes. The next nearest one is the Andromeda galaxy. That galaxy is two million light-years away from the Milky Way. It's a spiral galaxy, too. When we look at the Andromeda galaxy through a telescope, we get an idea of the shape of the Milky Way. With our biggest telescopes, we can see galaxies that are up to 100 million light-years away.

THIS IS JUST ONE HALF OF THE ANDROMEDA GALAXY.

## How do we "see" a galaxy with a radio telescope?

All stars shine with light. We can see that light with our eyes and with optical telescopes. But some stars also send out radio waves that are invisible. A radio telescope is a big, dish-shaped antenna, just like the ones some people use for TV reception. A motor turns the dish to point in every direction. The antenna catches radio waves from the stars of a galaxy, just as an optical telescope catches light.

The waves are sent to a computer that draws a map of the galaxy. To get a radio map as sharp as a picture from our biggest optical telescopes, we'd need a dish about 300 miles across! Since we can't build dishes that large, we use many smaller dishes hooked together. The largest radio telescope dish in use is in Arecibo, Puerto Rico. This dish is built between the walls of a valley. It's too big to be turned. Instead, the Arecibo dish turns along with the Earth each day to point at different parts of the sky.

*Are faraway galaxies in groups, too?*

Yes.  Just like the galaxies in our Local Swimming Hole,
distant galaxies are in groups called galaxy clusters.

*Are other galaxies about the same size as the
Milky Way?*

Anywhere from 10 million to 100 million light-years away. It can take up to 100 million years for light to come from a distant galaxy to Earth. Believe it or not, when we look at a distant galaxy through a telescope, we are seeing what the stars in that galaxy were doing 100 million years ago! Some of those stars might be old and burned out by now. Even the stars in our Milky Way galaxy are very far away from us. So when we see the stars at night, we are looking at starlight that started on its way to our eyes long, long ago.

*The light that we see tonight started on its way to our eyes millions of years ago.*

No, some are smaller, some larger. There is one distant galaxy that measures 10 million light-years across. That's more than three times bigger than the entire Local Swimming Hole!

## How else do galaxies differ?

They differ in shape.  Some are spiral galaxies, like the
Milky Way and Andromeda galaxies.

Others are called **elliptical galaxies**.  They look like a
ball that has been squeezed, so that it's no longer round.

And there's a third kind called **barred spiral galaxies**. They look like their name says—like a kind of fat, bright bar, with a spiral arm coming out of each end.

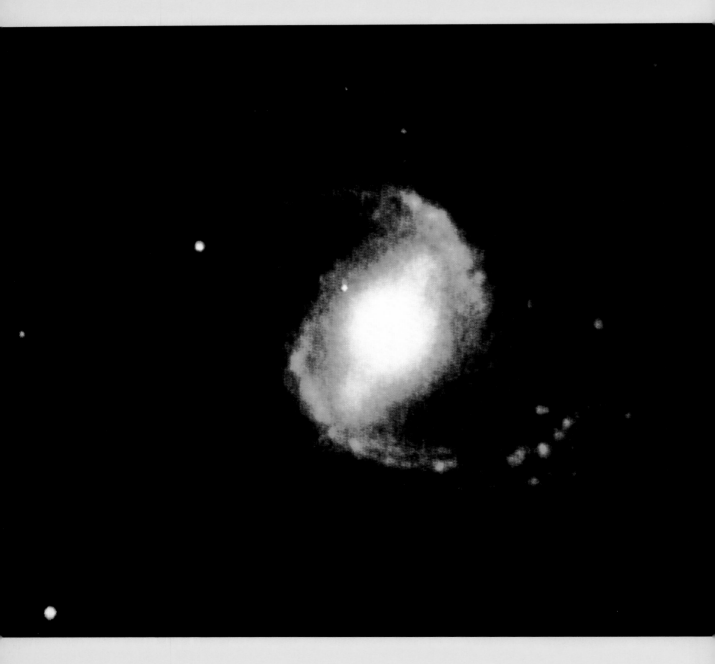

*Are those the only kinds of galaxy shapes?*

No. Some galaxies are just shapeless, like the Magellanic Clouds. They are called irregular galaxies.

And some have shapes that are kind of weird.

Others are like rings.

Look at the galaxy on the next page.  What kind of name would you give it?

If you think that it looks like a hat, you're right.
It's called the Sombrero galaxy!

*So getting to the Milky Way is easy,
isn't it?*

Not if you're living in another galaxy.
But for you on Earth, there's no problem.
You're part of the Milky Way already!

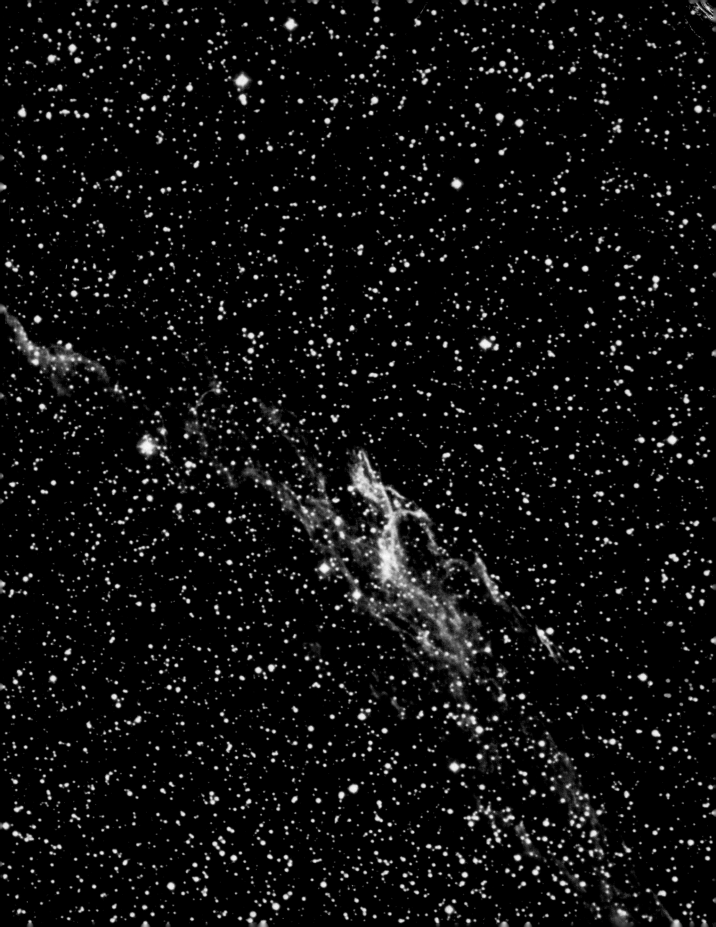

# GLOSSARY

**astronomer:** A scientist who is interested in explaining how the universe works, and who observes and studies planets, stars, and galaxies for that purpose

**barred spiral galaxies:** Spiral galaxies that have a thick line, or bar, of stars in the center

**elliptical galaxies:** Galaxies whose stars are clustered in a shape like a ball that's been squeezed out of shape

**galaxy:** A great collection of millions or billions of stars, gas, and dust held together by gravity. The Milky Way is our galaxy.

**gravity:** The force that makes objects attract each other. The Earth's gravity is so strong it keeps us stuck to Earth.

**light-year:** The distance a beam of light travels in one year, about six trillion miles

**Solar System:** The Sun and all the bodies that move around it—planets, moons, comets, asteroids, and meteors

**spiral galaxy:** A galaxy shaped like a pinwheel, with spiral arms turning around the center

**telescope:** An instrument used by astronomers to observe planets, stars, and galaxies